Take-Out Window

.

Take-Out Window

Haiku Society of America
2014 Members' Anthology

Gary Hotham
Editor

Haiku Society of America
New York

Take-Out Window

ISBN : 978-1-930172-12-8

Each poem in this anthology was selected by the editor from five published or unpublished haiku and senryu submitted by current members of the Haiku Society of America. Each participating member has one poem in this anthology.

Book Production: Éditions des petits nuages

All illustrations: Lidia Rozmus

Book cover design: Lidia Rozmus

Book layout: Lynda Wegner — www.freshimage.ca

Editor Comments

The yearly HSA members' anthology is an opportunity to have one's work appear with a variety of others in the English language haiku world. And so it was a fascinating experience to read the group of previously published or unpublished haiku that each member sent in. I hope I picked the haiku that represents your best moment.

Almost 300 members contributed. One thing that surprised me was the number of one-liners. All the rest were mostly three. Apparently two lines are either more difficult or just don't work well for the haiku. Maybe two lines are too much like a couplet. There are a couple examples.

I picked the title for the anthology from the haiku by Cor van den Heuvel. And not just because he is probably the oldest living practitioner of the genre to contribute to the anthology but it is a powerful image that captures modern life in a twinkling. I bet Cor wrote it slowly.

And a special thank you to Lidia Rozmus for allowing the anthology to use her sumi-e series, *The Point*, which add some delightful pizzazz for our naked eyes to the cover and the interior of the anthology. Yes, an art form that has to be done with bare hands.

Also thanks to David Lanoue for his help— and especially the opportunity he gave me to edit the anthology for this year. Also thanks to Mike Montreuil and Michael Dylan Welch for their suggestions and help in the process.

As the reader will soon note the haiku are not alphabetical by last name. So those who are usually last or first won't find themselves so easily. The order is not random. There was a method to their placement. I wouldn't go out of my way to determine the algorithm I used since I don't think it will bring any more enjoyment as you read thru the anthology and there is no prize if you do recover it!

May it be a pleasant read for you.

Gary Hotham
9/11 Thirteen Years On

same old accusations
the winter sky
staring back

Mark Forrester
Hyattsville, Maryland

boardwalk rain
a wet ketchup bottle
at the take-out window

Cor van den Heuvel
New York, New York

waning moon
the "hey" to "hello"
then silence

Dorothy Coraggio
Palm City, Florida

moonless night
the idea of someone
I won't see again

Miloje Savic
Oslo, Norway

grape leaves
her hands as I fold them
across her chest

Johnette Downing
New Orleans, Louisiana

new home—
at night I dream
of another place

Edith Bartholomeusz
Phoenix, Arizona

spring again
the winos reclaim
their benches

Gary Simpson
Fairview Heights, Illinois

against
the blue
the blue
fly flies
against
the pane

jim kacian
Winchester, Virginia

just a little ahead
of my shadow
autumn loneliness

Kath Abela Wilson
Pasadena, California

a sound on the air
arouses my loneliness
the cry of a loon

Marian Schwilk-Thomas
Vandalia, Ohio

awoke alive
from the record grooves
our long past springtime

Eiko Yachimoto
Yokosuka City, Kanagawa, Japan

dining alone
the piped-in music plays
our love song

Victor P. Gendrano
Seal Beach, California

after the argument
separating
lights and darks

Kristen Deming
Bethesda, Maryland

under the ash
leaving before the rain
really stops

David Jacobs
London, United Kingdom

scattered ashes—
the things
I don't remember

Seren Fargo
Bellingham, Washington

his third autumn
when all squash
are pumpkins

Jim Laurila
Florence, Massachusetts

weaving into woods   our path circles back

Edward J. Rielly
Westbrook, Maine

after a bath
the lingering warmth
fades to pianissimo

Lori Zajkowski
New York, New York

heat lightning in the dusk waves of bats

Dan Daly
Ballwin, Missouri

the beach
where her ashes were strewn
waves caress my feet

Diane Wallihan
Port Townsend, Washington

left on a park bench
wildflowers
and children's laughter

Rich Burke
Limerick, Pennsylvania

pause between
winter and spring
old horse sniffs the air

Laureen McHugh
Simsbury, Connecticut

in the roadside bin
other people's
New Year resolutions

John Kinory
Steeple Aston, Oxfordshire, England

bindweed
along the road . . .
I thought he was special

Pamela Larson
Arlington Heights, Illinois

this morning's sorrow drowned by the birds

Denise Fontaine-Pincince
Belchertown, Massachusetts

even in winter rain her blondsong

Robert Epstein
Los Angeles, California

cherry blossoms . . .
she asks me to bury her
in pink

Terri L. French
Huntsville, Alabama

onion snow
even the paired geese
bewildered

Matthew Caretti
Mercersburg, Pennsylvania

first cherry blossom
on a package from Japan—
I put away the quilts

Angelee Deodhar
Chandigarh, U.T., India

Late night fades to blue
Hourglass nefarious
Shadows dim needles.

Wilson F. Engel III
Gilbert, Arizona

not yet born
but already present
in the whole house

Klaus-Dieter Wirth
Viersen, NRW, Germany

Glacial boulders
growing mossy beards
a long winter.

John-Carl Davis
West Bend, Wisconsin

a black box
now we are happy
to have any news

Olga Skvortsova
Beijing, China

the sinewy boughs
of the ancient oak;
firewood sale

Dean S. Uyeno
Mount Juliet, Tennessee

my daughter's visit
the pomegranate
we didn't buy

Brenda Lempp
Madison, Wisconsin

braiding
silence into dreams . . .
full moon

Rita Odeh
Nazareth, Israel

autumn breeze
leaves fall everywhere
Basho's grave

William Seltzer
Gwynedd, Pennsylvania

since the burial
her garden overrun with
forget-me-nots

Lori Becherer
Millstadt, Illinois

hurricane bulletin
my pot of soup
boils over

Merle D. Hinchee
Houma, Louisiana

17

her call—
the loneliness
in a voice

Mike Montreuil
Ottawa, Ontario, Canada

the security camera
pans the sky
round August moon

Dianne Garcia
Seattle, Washington

campground
I use a pine needle
for a bookmark

deanna tiefenthal
Rochester, New York

carillon
melody changing
with the wind

Valorie Broadhurst Woerdehoff
Dubuque, Iowa

carousel
beyond my grasp
the brass ring

Renee Londner
Prospect, Connecticut

night
the gingko shudders
goldening the ground

Robert Witmer
Tokyo, Japan

her empty chair . . .
still telling
old ghost stories

Amelia Cotter
Chicago, Illinois

by chance
the universe
spring blossoms

James Won
Temple City, California

chives
the first bite
of spring

Deb Koen
Rochester, New York

in the darkened church
one quarter of the quartet
rehearses

Marcyn Clements
Claremont, California

cold winter day
alone in the coffee house
— I switch chairs

Steven H. Greene
Haddon Twp, New Jersey

not a color
I'd ever wear
azaleas

Kate MacQueen
Chapel Hill, North Carolina

23

the clarity
of all essence—
a cat's purr

Jeffrey Winke
Milwaukee, Wisconsin

mum's closet
the March of Dimes folder
half-filled

Richard St. Clair
Cambridge, Massachusetts

chilly evening commute
Amtrak and Beethoven
blending horns

James L Davis
Silver Spring, Maryland

city street corner
    icy wind,   leafless plants
        Picasso faces,   on garden shed

Johnathan Ericson
Philadelphia, Pennsylvania

watercolor class—
we lay our brushes down
at sunset

Ruth Holzer
Herndon, Virginia

thirteen cranes
the city skyline
readjusts

William Scott Galasso
Edmonds, Washington

subzero creak
of the door opened a crack
valentine's day

Elizabeth Hazen
Williston, Vermont

coyote's cry
hangs in the desert night
no reply

E. Luke
Los Angeles, California

lone cumulus
swallows a star
spits it out again

Doris Lynch
Bloomington, Indiana

endless rain . . .
mother's silver beginning
to tarnish

Margaret Dornaus
Ozark, Arkansas

twisted and curled
racing across hillsides
willow leaves

V.A. Fleming
Little Rock, Arkansas

cold Sunday dawn
someone's put a love poem
in the classifieds

Janelle Barrera
Key West, Florida

all souls' day
no one i care
to see again

Roberta Beary
Bethesda, Maryland

another friend dead . . .
a boy pours tadpoles
into the stream

Ferris Gilli
Marietta, Georgia

recording her death
leaves of other autumns
fall from the pages

Del Todey Turner
Waterloo, Iowa

warm December
I circle the new lump
in green

Glenn G. Coats
Prospect, Virginia

zero degrees
beside the doughnut shop
a dozen glazed cars

Ginny Hoyle
Denver, Colorado

all along the undergrowth beads of dew

Dina E Cox
Unionville, Ontario, Canada

her diagnosis
through cut glass
        peonies fall

John Parsons
Norfolk, UK

nighthawks diving
this dark not the same
as that dark

Cherie Hunter Day
Cupertino, California

Out the door
Down the steps
Dog meets ice.

Ron Grognet
New Orleans, Louisiana

just a sliver of moon seeds my doubt

Renée Owen
Sebastopol, California

June downpour
my heart follows
the funeral procession

Polly Swafford
Prairie Village, Kansas

while we dreamed
a lily bloomed
in the gift bouquet

William Hart
Montrose, California

dancing droplets
on the windshield
at the car wash

Joanne M. Hogan
Byfield, Massachusetts

early morning breeze—
a little girl's dream
stirs the wishing well

Poppy Herrin
Gonzales, Louisiana

preening for Easter
the family
of rabbits

Michael B. Schoenburg
Skokie, Illinois

at the water's edge
'mid the disappearing mist
cherry blossoms fall

Patricia Noeth
Iowa City, Iowa

wind the sound of all else

Joseph Salvatore Aversano
Ankara, Turkey

a lattice of spent cucumber vines summer's end

James A. Paulson
Narberth, Pennsylvania

big enough
for coyote howls
winter sky

Chandra Bales
Albuquerque, New Mexico

New Year's Eve
a broken bough holds on
to the snow

Michele Root-Bernstein
East Lansing, Michigan

everything
out of balance except
this morning's snow

Rich Schnell
Port Douglas, New York

fallen blossoms . . .
a grey haired servant sweeping
at twilight

Sandip Chauhan
Great Falls, Virginia

her everywhere . . .
a slender-eyed photo
spread in Vogue

Thomas Chockley
Plainfield, Illinois

lighting their faces
stories around the fire

Simon Hanson
Allendale, SA, Australia

A leaf falling . . .
no child
to catch it

Robert F. Mainone
Delton, Michigan

fathoming
from the twelfth floor
the deadly distance

Max Verhart
Den Bosch, Netherlands

fall breeze
my small son hunched
over fractions

Lesley Clinton
Sugar Land, Texas

36

fireflies
parked on the lawn
police cars

good ~

      Jimmy the Peach (Jim Aaron)
      Arlington, Virginia

       summer night—
       through the screen door
       the sounds of kids hiding

           Timothy I. Mize
           Yukon, Oklahoma

night fishing
words splashing
in this spring rain

      Claudia Chapline
      Stinson Beach, California

river in flood
telling him more
than he wants to know

Susan Constable
Nanoose Bay, British Columbia, Canada

fog . . .
fog . . . HORN
fog . . .

Mike Taylor
San Francisco, California

watching the garden
quiet into darkness—
everyone else shopping

CR Manley
Bellevue, Washington

the way I fondle
her neck
my blue Fender

Haiku Elvis (Carlos Colón)
Shreveport, Louisiana

whispers of a fragrance
my sister loved
evening in spring

Ellen Compton
Washington, DC

spinning free
of the trick roper's lasso
dust devil

Chad Lee Robinson
Pierre, South Dakota

death of a friend
the empty moon stoke
still in my brush

Ron C. Moss
Tasmania, Australia

first frost
both sides
of the fallen leaf

Gretchen Graft Batz
Elsah, Illinois

November rain
on black umbrellas—
that song about Camelot

Mary Frederick Ahearn
Pottstown, Pennsylvania

a little fuzzy
about the meaning of grace
scent of apriums

Beverly Acuff Momoi
Mountain View, California

winter galaxy—
a younger me once resolved
there'd be no regrets

Patricia J. Machmiller
San Jose, California

November garden
Ancient azalea
One bud unopened

Marilyn Gabel
Agawam, Massachusetts

Demoiselle geese
wing their farewells
to chilly autumn.

Suzanne Vacany Surles
Jacksonville, North Carolina

spring geese—
hoping for a quick resale
we paint the front door

Elizabeth Howard
Crossville, Tennessee

sea glass
the edges of an old hurt
smoothed by time

Catherine J.S. Lee
Eastport, Maine

overnight snowfall
a cat's
footprints

Joan W Rossi
Haverhill, Massachusetts

ducks glide
in the no-wake zone
sundown

Ida Freilinger
Bellevue, Washington

morning glories
remembering
my parents having coffee

Celia Stuart-Powles
Tulsa, Oklahoma

winter night
the tremor of his hand
against my back

Patricia Harvey
East Longmeadow, Massachusetts

a glow
in dusk's shadows
—blue delphinium

Victoria Witherow
Salt Lake City, Utah

northern graveyard
the tiny sweetness
of wild strawberries

Jeanne Jorgensen
Edmonton, Alberta, Canada

Hoping that Earl Grey
Will warm and release the muse
The tea pot boils dry . . .

Paul S. Nash
Malibu, California

sacred ground
red geraniums
where they fell

Ernest J Berry
Blenheim, New Zealand

a new blue hat
for the seventh decade
autumn sunrise

Bruce H. Feingold
Berkeley, California

desert highway
the clouds
lost in my thoughts

Oleg Kagan
Los Angeles, California

Earth's spongy hillsides
Weep winter waters, melding
In swift, swollen streams.

Mollie Danforth
Alexandria, Virginia

lingering with him . . .
i watch the wind scatter
his ashes

Charlotte Digregorio
Winnetka, Illinois

jostling the hive
a swarm
of cherry petals

Sidney Bending
Victoria, British Columbia, Canada

over every autumn hill my childhood home

Bonnie Stepenoff
Cape Girardeau, Missouri

my father's house
the path we used to walk
softened by moss

Marcus Liljedahl
Gothenburg, Sweden

roads draped in ice
the winter she slipped
away

S.M. Kozubek
Chicago, Illinois

Basho's Unreal Hut
sound of his drinking stream
all that's left

Bruce Ross
Hampden, Maine

labyrinth . . .
I slow to the pace
of the snail

Carole MacRury
Point Roberts, Washington

foggy autumn lake . . .
an occasional ripple
to break the silence

brett brady
Pahoa, Hawaii

hanging her laundry
slighter still
my mother's limbs

Sharon Pretti
San Francisco, California

flaming leaves . . .
they speak
in tongues

Jennifer Thiermann
Glenview, Illinois

leaving
the cancer center
rain, then hail

Mary Jo Balistreri
Genesee Depot, Wisconsin

my letter
never answered
walking rain

Alanna C. Burke
Santa Fe, New Mexico

counting open lids
on the pill box
it's Wednesday

Caroline Giles Banks
Minneapolis, Minnesota

my modest life
after coastal redwoods
the pines back home

> *Kathe L. Palka*
> *Flemington, New Jersey*

all day loneliness . . .
pulling apart
a plum blossom

> *Stanford M. Forrester*
> *Windsor, Connecticut*

redbud rain—
as if the robins
needed an excuse

> *Mike W. Blottenberger*
> *Hanover, Pennsylvania*

increasingly lost
on familiar trails
reveries

William F. Schnell
Aurora, Ohio

lullaby
no other word
will do

Lynne Rees
Offham, Kent, UK

mission to mars
one red and one yellow
rain boot

Michael Henry Lee
Saint Augustine, Florida

snowmelt
everything flows
through my old porch

Merrill Ann Gonzales
Dayville, Connecticut

our mixed messages
the woodpecker tapping
his own code

Elizabeth Fanto
Timonium, Maryland

the sea mist
rolling in at Ninilchik—
almost home

Connie Hutchison
Kirkland, Washington

a monarch
graces the crown of my head
butterfly house

Mary Kipps
Sterling, Virginia

crescent moon
magnolia petals
scoop it up

Suzanne Niedzielska
Glastonbury, Connecticut

gray morning
taking the rainbow with him
cayuga drake

Marie Louise Munro
Tarzana, California

in the soft, still morning
pink oleanders . . .
causing a riot

Cheryl Anderson
Kenilworth, Illinois

dead moth
on the windowsill
wings fluttering

Scott Wiggerman
Austin, Texas

mountains
we climbed yesterday
only clouds today

Sheila Sondik
Bellingham, Washington

after the movie
in his old Chevy
confessions

Peggy Hale Bilbro
Huntsville, Alabama

strangely moving~
run-on words
no dash

Ann M. Penton
Green Valley, Arizona

disturbed by night
tangle of tumbleweeds
gone with the wind

Barbara Tate
Winchester, Tennessee

a joyous noise
from reeds near the creek—
chorus frogs

Art Elser
Denver, Colorado

high noon . . .
a child chalks an outline
around my shadow

S.M. Abeles
Washington, DC

she loves me . . . not
I gather the petals
for a potpourri

George Dorsty
Yorktown, Virginia

a passed note
do you like me or not
my paper heart

Susan Burch
Hagerstown, Maryland

rainy night . . .
our conversation
circling the drain

Lolly Williams
Santa Clarita, California

nostalgia
billowing with sea wind
my summer dress

Maxianne Berger
Outremont, Quebec, Canada

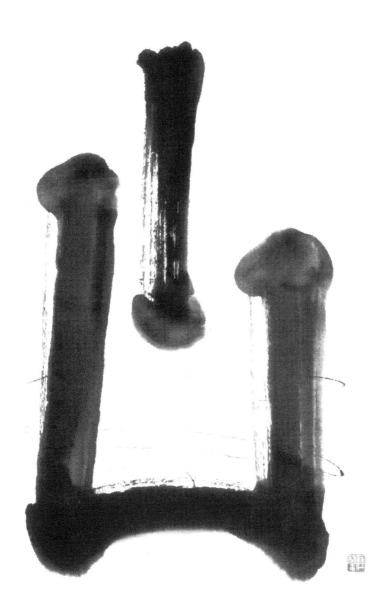

rose oleander
lines every byway
~a breeze to take home

Anne Hatley
Albany, Oregon

old arguments . . .
the purple-edged leaves
of thai basil

Deborah P Kolodji
Temple City, California

my ashes
won't be me—
winter oaks

David G. Lanoue
New Orleans, Louisiana

open a window on snowmelt in the mountains ominous

Francis Attard
Marsa, Malta

putting on
the same clothes as yesterday—
new year's morning

Ce Rosenow
Eugene, Oregon

drizzle off and on . . .
walking home from the Herb Fair
with a flat of herbs

Robert Gilliland
Austin, Texas

reaching out
my arms carve from fog
two long scars

Ellen Peckham
New York, New York

I overlook
what I think I know . . .
robin song

Michele L. Harvey
Hamilton, New York

open page
  shadow of the poem
    leans forward

Karen DiNobile
Poughkeepsie, New York

twice past
the same buoy
catfish in a pail

LeRoy Gorman
Napanee, Ontario, Canada

On the path
by the chorus frogs
a man's whistle

Shelley Baker-Gard
Portland, Oregon

city park—
violin notes
the color of sunset

Jay Friedenberg
New York, New York

On the patio
Morning drifts along
With cicada sounds

Mary Ann Newkirk
Greer, South Carolina

perfectly
white clouds on blue sky
painted china

Leanne McIntosh
Nanaimo, British Columbia, Canada

Persephone
Waters her roses
amidst the thorns

Ralph Moritz
Ballwin, Missouri

petunia
wishing it could be
a tuba

RaNae Merrill
New York, New York

Lego pieces
Scattered, fragmented
Childhood memories

Neal T Williams
Arvada, Colorado

lettuce plants
under a green tarp;
mother's day snow

Joan Cheng
Boulder, Colorado

the record player
skips at the end—
mourning doves coo

Roy Kindelberger
Bothell, Washington

farm pond . . .
muskrats chase
their own ripples

Julie Warther
Dover, Ohio

prayers
scattered with her ashes
mountain chill

Johnnie Johnson Hafernik
San Francisco, California

morning prayer
water birds flying north
stay close to water

Ellen Grace Olinger
Oostburg, Wisconsin

art print
behind bars of winter light
Vincent's flowers

Catherine Anne Nowaski
Rochester, New York

between fence rails
a little boy explains cows
to the cows

Marsh Muirhead
Bemidji, Minnesota

after the rain
strings of sky between
rows of beans

Brad Bennett
Arlington, Massachusetts

yellow light turns red
racing
to the meditation group

Mac Greene
Indianapolis, Indiana

watering the new redbud
with peppermint tea
winter drought

Tricia Knoll
Portland, Oregon

71

Squirrel reparations
for stolen seeds, nuts, bird feed—
this butternut squash.

Donald Fry
Lansdowne, Pennsylvania

newborn baby no batteries required

John Quinnett
Bryson City, North Carolina

yesterdays in my cup near the rim

Gloria Ayvazian
Northampton, Massachusetts

rising
with the light
lilac breeze

Ann K. Schwader
Westminster, Colorado

homebound road
a rainbow
to some place

Dietmar Tauchner
Puchberg, Austria

the scene so much sadder
set in autumn
rice vinegar

Angela Terry
Lake Forest Park, Washington

rummage sale
all the seasons
in one bag

Barbara Snow
Eugene, Oregon

the Seven Samurai
could not have saved it
Hiroshima

Johnny Baranski
Vancouver, Washington

thesaurus search:
so few words
for goodbye

Lew Watts
Santa Fe, New Mexico

consolation in each raindrop the sea

Stella Pierides
Neusaess, Germany

in the morning air
my neighbor's wisteria
welcomes spring

Janis Albright Lukstein
Los Angeles, California

changing season
the stick in the window
sideways

Jeffrey McMullen
Cuba, New York

secrets
tucked in
full moon

Karen O'Leary
West Fargo, North Dakota

dandelion seeds
rising up from center field
with the gloved line drive

Phil Allen
Hartland, Wisconsin

afternoon shadow
under the funeral home tent
daddy's survivors

L. Teresa Church
Durham, North Carolina

76

no one to see spilled coffee heart shaped

Phyllis Lee
Sebring, Ohio

Still shining
over the old pond
light from a fallen star

Sylvia Forges-Ryan
North Haven, Connecticut

gate blown shut
by the winter wind
broken promise

Dennise Aiello
Benton, Louisiana

a handheld sign—
a light breeze
riffles the tall grass

Dean Summers
Seattle, Washington

Maple leaves skitter
across Post Office floor—
Santa Ana winds

Larry Barber
Ventura, California

thickening sky
the scent from the soup pot
gathers us in

Margaret D. McGee
Port Townsend, Washington

I wake to the smell
of someone's sorrow
wildfire

Gregory Longenecker
Pasadena, California

snowbound
the pine cone opens
in my hand

Jeannie Martin
Arlington, Massachusetts

the sound
of waves on waves
how did I get middle aged

Bryan Hansel
Grand Marais, Minnesota

february snow
falls in whispers—
unwelcomed guest

Andrea Vlahakis
Woodbury, Connecticut

spring sortie
forgetting how it sounded
before the geese

Autumn Noelle Hall
Green Mountain Falls, Colorado

evening star . . .
the cornhusker
brushes back her hair

Gwenn Gurnack
Boston, Massachusetts

the longest day
cucumber and squash blossoms
intermingle

Marilyn Appl Walker
Madison, Georgia

first steps—
the baby laughs like her
grandmother

Carmel Lively Westerman
Yuma, Arizona

A stone
takes its shadow
into the water

Bruce England
Santa Clara, California

May Day—
the things I took for granted
like bare upper arms

Judith Morrison Schallberger
San Jose, California

end of summer . . .
the ping of a grasshopper
in an empty pail

Elinor Pihl Huggett
Lakeville, Indiana

sycamores
of Sycamore Street
the echo

Michael Fessler
Sagamihara, Kanagawa, Japan

two more sympathy
cards arrive . . .
the day's drizzle

Joan Prefontaine
Cottonwood, Arizona

cotton sweater
nothing prepared me for
this final phase

Michael Sheffield
Kenwood, California

early fall—the silence of a porch swing

Padma Thampatty
Wexford, Pennsylvania

the small talk
of strangers—
water striders

Carolyn Coit Dancy
Pittsford, New York

a jar of sun tea
steeping in the garden—
Independence Day

Carolyn M. Hinderliter
Phoenix, Arizona

spring thaw . . .
lost glove
by the sidewalk

Tomoko Hata
Winnetka, Illinois

wandering through
my daydream slowly—
time on my toes

Carole Ann Lovin
Clearwater, Florida

wood thrush
his longing
just music

Jeff Hoagland
Hopewell, New Jersey

thunderbumpers
cloud shadows on
the desert floor

Andrea Eldridge
Claremont, California

low tide . . .
a cello solo brings
the edge of panic

Marylouise Knight
Omaha, Nebraska

Eve ning stac ca to
choose me no choose me no choose
summer drifts away

R Michael Beatty
South Bend, Indiana

his lapis toenails
my brother's last breath

Belle Shalom
Bellingham, Washington

green tomato—
the one raccoons
missed

jill (Jill Lange)
Cleveland Heights, Ohio

after the tornado
we carefully listen for
bird and cricket calls

Peg McAulay Byrd
Madison, New Jersey

quiet morning no slug at the end of the slug's trail

Bob Lucky
Addis Ababa, Ethiopia

after transplanting
bleeding hearts into the earth
a blood moon

Margaret Chula
Portland, Oregon

traveling alone
I share a cab
with perfume

Ann Magyar
Brighton, Massachusetts

skeleton trees
white sky at dawn
nothing to end silence

Jim Applegate
Roswell, New Mexico

twilight
one echo
light

Gary Hotham
Scaggsville, Maryland

sermon unwritten
the noise
of the de-humidifier

Bruce J. Pfeffer
Indianapolis, Indiana

we, too, will vanish
if we move into this fog—
owl song

Billie Wilson
Juneau, Alaska

they once brought us here our chip wrappers soaked in vinegar

frances angela
London, United Kingdom

after your visit
our chairs still turned
toward each other

Donna Bauerly
Dubuque, Iowa

skies softening for now wait-listed

Jeff Stillman
Norwich, New York

brick walkway
last night's elusive
dream

Scott Glander
Glenview, Illinois

on the office wall
a calendar
waits for Monday

Peter Butler
London, England

dementia ward
a broken clock
on the wall

Beverly Bachand
Summerville, South Carolina

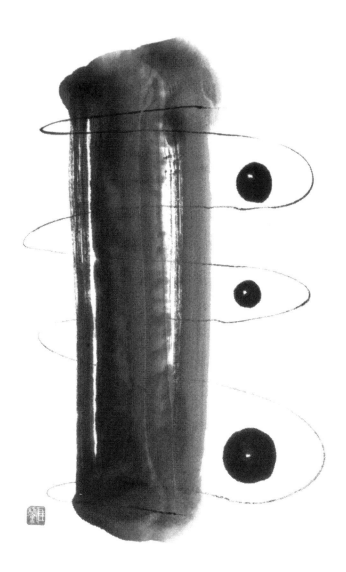

stone walls
separate living from dead . . .
orange lichen

Sue Richards
Birmingham, United Kingdom

weathervane
shifting atop the horse barn
pigeon shadows

Marilyn Fleming
Pewaukee, Wisconsin

our daughter's wedding
dusting the room
she dreamed in

Francine Banwarth
Dubuque, Iowa

dead now two weeks
and still I try to save
his paw print in the mud

Arch Haslett
Toronto, Ontario, Canada

singing a while
without realizing it . . .
The Pleiades

Brent Goodman
Rhinelander, Wisconsin

the dog whines
on both sides of the door
spring rain

Karen Stromberg
La Mesa, California

Whippoorwill
and firefly
in-sync to the glow.

Wesley D. Willis
Eldon, Missouri

whispering
sweet nothings
all he had

Kevin Goldstein-Jackson
Poole, Dorset, England

all winter
waiting . . .
for winter

Susan Godwin
Madison, Wisconsin

99

so many wishes
the weight
of a dandelion

Annette Makino
Arcata, California

winter woman
remembering
spring woman

Helen A. Granger
Corunna, Michigan

the local wren—
building her nest up inside
the metal heron

Rick Clark
Ocean Shores, Washington

a new year—
one more pill
to swallow

John J. Han
Manchester, Missouri

awakened by rain-soaked dawn, and you
                              warm behind me

Marian Olson
Santa Fe, New Mexico

winter afternoon
transferring slivers of soap
to a different dish

Sheila K. Barksdale
Gainesville, Florida

spring again
the cemetery
pays me a visit

David Gershator
St. Thomas, Virgin Islands

plum blossoms
the heart of the matter
eludes us

Carolyn Hall
San Francisco, California

morning breeze~
ironing out
the new shirt's crease

Bill Deegan
Mahwah, New Jersey

cicada husk my faith in chance

Tom Painting
Atlanta, Georgia

scanning stars
another arm around
another neck

Ralf Bröker
Ochtrup, NRW, Germany

Memorial Day
who will cherish his things
when she's gone?

Steve Hodge
White Lake, Michigan

spring downpour
the puddles return
to their places

Roland Packer
Hamilton, Ontario, Canada

snow falling
on tangled trees
alone with my thoughts

Susan B. Auld
Arlington Heights, Illinois

a walled garden
ancient bonsai
peek through the fog

Jack Douthitt
Fox Point, Wisconsin

walk around the house
from sunny side to the shade
smell of wet paint

Walt Mehring
Hanover, Pennsylvania

raking leaves
the things I wish
I'd said

Joe McKeon
Strongsville, Ohio

spring melt
all my regrets
pulled out to sea

Michael Rehling
Presque Isle, Michigan

105

oh monarch,
I too want to wander
over earth over water

Marilyn Shoemaker Hazelton
Allentown, Pennsylvania

crescent moon
a new row
at Arlington

Wanda D. Cook
Hadley, Massachusetts

Summer mountain:
morning mist
the only sound

Dave Sutter
San Francisco, California

nightfall
the silhouette
of a dove

June Rose Dowis
Shreveport, Louisiana

i shed the skin in one piece
winter orange

Carole E. Slesnick
Bellingham, Washington

koi pond
removing the weight
of my backpack

Ben Moeller-Gaa
St. Louis, Missouri

lily pond
white clouds fill
open water

Katherine Raine Milton
Otago, New Zealand

summer rain
filling the sidewalk cracks
mother's birthday

Phillip Kennedy
Monterey, California

yard sale—
a row of empty jars
tinged slightly red

Michael Dylan Welch
Sammamish, Washington

hurricane season
the childhood nickname
you didn't foresee

Christina Nguyen
Hugo, Minnesota

Butterfly's shadow
Traces a route no straighter
Down the garden path

Robert Forsythe
Annandale, Virginia

nearly summer—
the mirror
shows a woman

Nicholas M. Sola
New Orleans, Louisiana

low winter sun
my fingers probe
the empty birdhouse

paul m.
Bristol, Rhode Island

they are talking
about me—
quivering aspen

Mimi Ahern
San Jose, California

unexpected thaw
the tilted pinwheel
begins to spin

Lesley Anne Swanson
Coopersburg, Pennsylvania

on tip-toes
watching me wash
an apple

D.W. Skrivseth
St. Anthony, Minnesota

family grave visit
the sunset
hovers over it

Carolyn Noah Graetz
New Orleans, Louisiana

Navy Day
the new perfumes
of sailors' wives

Michael McClintock
Clovis, California

long winter
red berries in the corner
of my eye

Mary Ellen Rooney
New York, New York

home alone
ticking
of my pulse

Lidia Rozmus
Vernon Hills, Illinois

PUBLICATION CREDITS

Some of haiku were first published in other media. The following from information provided by the authors.

S.M. Abeles: *Frogpond*, 36.3, 2013
Phil Allen: *Notes from the Gean*, No. 13, June 2012
Frances Angela: *Blithe Spirit,* 24.2, 2014
Francis Attard: *Frogpond*, 33:1, 2010
Susan B. Auld: *Modern Haiku*, 44.2, 2013
Chandra Bales: *The Shiki Monthly Kukai*, December
        2010, third place
Francine Banwarth: *The Heron's Nest*, 15:3, 2013
Gretchen Graft Batz: *South by Southeast*, 18:1, 2011
Donna Bauerly: *Frogpond*, 35:2, 2012
Roberta Beary: *Frogpond,* 37:1, 2014
Sidney Bending: Vancouver Cherry Blossom Festival
        2013, Sakura Award
Brett Brady: *Haiku Journal*, 3:1, 1979
Susan Burch: *Writers and Lovers Café*, Spring 2014
Lesley Clinton: *Frogpond*, 36:4, 2014
Ellen Compton: *playing a lullaby:* The Betty Drevniok
        Awards, 2012
Susan Constable: *Modern Haiku*, 44:3, 2013
Carolyn Coit Dancy: *Mayfly,* 56, 2014
Bill Deegan: *Bottle Rockets*, 14:2, 2013
Kristen Deming: *Frogpond*, 34:3, 2011
Karen DiNobile: *Frogpond*, 36:1, 2013
Margaret Dornaus: *The Heron's Nest*, 15:3, 2013
George Dorsty: *Bottle Rockets*, Summer, 2013
Seren Fargo: *Mu Haiku Journal*, The 7's Contest, 2011,
        1st Place
Marilyn Fleming: *Dragonfly: East/West Haiku*
        Quarterly, 15:1, 1989
Sylvia Forges-Ryan: *Frogpond*, 34:2, 2011
Mark Forrester: *Bottle Rockets*, 15.1, 2013
William Scott Galasso: *Hummingbird,* Dec. 2013

David Gershator: *Frogpond*, 35:2, 2012
Ferris Gilli: *Acorn*, 21, 2008
LeRoy Gorman: *Tinywords*, 13:2, 2013
Helen A. Granger: *Frogpond*, 36:2, 2013
Gwenn Gurnack: *Frogpond*, 36:2, 2013
Johnnie Johnson Hafernik: *Modern Haiku*, 43:3, 2012
Gary Hotham: 18th Kusamakura Haiku Competition,
    Tokusen Award, 2013
Arch Haslett: *Haiku Canada Review*, 7:1, 2013
Jim Kacian: *Tinywords,* 14.1, 2014
John Kinory: *Kô,* 4, 2008
S.M. Kozubek: *Frogpond*, 35:2, 2012
Bob Lucky: *Modern Haiku*, 42.3, 2011
Patricia J. Machmiller: *Frogpond*, 36:2, 2013
Robert F. Mainone: *An Anthology of Haiku by People of
    the United States and Canada*, 1988
Jeannie Martin: *Clear Water*, Red Moon Publications,
    Oklahoma City, OK, 2013
Margaret D. McGee: *Frogpond,* 36:2, 2013
Beverly Acuff Momoi: *Modern Haiku*, 44:3, 2013
Ron C. Moss: *Bottle Rockets*, 29, 2013
Marsh Muirhead: *The Heron's Nest,* 11:1, 2009
Patricia Noeth: *Lyrical Iowa*, 2010
Rita Odeh: *Back to Hokku*, 25 February 2014
Ellen Grace Olinger: *SMILE,* 67, 2012
Marian Olson: *Haiku Quarterly*, 1:1, 1989
Renée Owen: *Modern Haiku*, 45.2, 2014
Roland Packer: *Kokako*, 16, 2012
Tom Painting: *Modern Haiku,* 44:1, 2013
Kathe L. Palka: *Bottle Rockets*, 30, 2013
John Parsons: *Kokako*, 15, 2011
James A. Paulson: *Bottle Rockets,* 8:2, 2007
Bruce J. Pfeffer: *Modern Haiku*, 42:3, 2011
Stella Pierides: TW, 14.1, 2014
Michael Rehling: *A Hundred Gourds*, 2:4, 2013
Chad Lee Robinson: *Bottle Rockets*, 30, 2014
Miloje Savic: *Frogpond*, 37:1, 2013

Richard St. Clair: *Frogpond,* 37:1, 2013
Ann K. Schwader: *A Hundred Gourds,* 1.1, 2011
William Seltzer: *Haiku International,* 107, 2013
Gary Simpson: *Frogpond,* 36:2, 2013
Jeff Stillman: *Acorn,* 31, 2013
Karen Stromberg: *dandelion breeze,* Southern California
       Haiku Group Anthology, 2013
Dave Sutter: *Modern Haiku,* 23:2, 1992
Lesley Anne Swanson: The Haiku Calendar Competition
       2014, Snapshot Press
Barbara Tate: *Frogpond,* 35:3, 2012
Dietmar Tauchner: *Presence,* 49, 2014
Cor van den Heuvel: *Suspiciously Small,* The Spring
       Street Haiku Group, 2010
Andrea Vlahakis: *South by Southeast,* 4:2, 1997
Marilyn Appl Walker: *Valley Voices,* Mississippi Valley
       State University, spring, 2008
Lew Watts: *Modern Haiku,* 44.2, 2013
Kath Abela Wilson: *Modern Haiku,* 45:1, 2013

Illustrations

Illustrations are from the sumi-e series, "The Point," by Lidia Rozmus:

Index of Poets

Blottenberger, Mike W., 53
brady, brett, 51
Bröker, Ralf, 103
Burch, Susan, 60
Burke, Alanna C., 52
Burke, Rich, 11
Butler, Peter, 93
Byrd, Peg McAulay, 89
Caretti, Matthew, 14
Chapline, Claudia, 37
Chauhan, Sandip, 35
Cheng, Joan, 68
Chockley, Thomas, 35
Chula, Margaret, 90
Church, L. Teresa, 76
Clark, Rick, 100
Clements, Marcyn, 23
Clinton, Lesley, 36
Coats, Glenn G., 29
Colón, Carlos, 41
Compton, Ellen, 41
Constable, Susan, 38
Cook, Wanda D., 106
Coraggio, Dorothy, 5
Cotter, Amelia, 22
Cox, Dina E, 29
Daly, Dan, 11
Dancy, Carolyn Coit, 86
Danforth, Mollie, 48
Davis, James L., 24
Davis, John-Carl, 15
Day, Cherie Hunter, 30
Deegan, Bill, 102
Deming, Kristen B., 9
Deodhar, Angelee, 14
Digregorio, Charlotte, 48

DiNobile, Karen, 65
Dornaus, Margaret, 27
Dortsy, George, 59
Douthitt, Jack, 104
Dowis, June Rose, 107
Downing, Johnette, 6
Eldridge, Andrea, 87
Elser, Art, 59
Engel III, Wison F., 14
England, Bruce, 83
Epstein, Robert, 13
Ericson, Johnathan, 25
Fanto, Elizabeth, 55
Fargo, Seren, 9
Feingold, Bruce H., 47
Fessler, Michael, 84
Fleming, Marilyn, 97
Fleming, V.A., 27
Fontaine-Pincince, Denise, 13
Forges-Ryan, Sylvia, 77
Forrester, Mark, 5
Forrester, Stanford M., 53
Forsythe, Robert, 109
Freilinger, Ida M., 45
French, Terri L., 13
Friedenberg, Jay, 66
Fry, Donald, 72
Gabel, Marilyn, 43
Galasso, William Scott, 25
Garcia, Dianne, 18
Gendrano, Victor P., 8
Gershator, David, 102
Gilli, Ferris, 28
Gilliland, Robert, 64
Glander, Scott, 93
Godwin, Susan, 99

Goldstein-Jackson, Kevin, 99
Gonzales, Merrill Ann, 55
Goodman, Brent, 98
Gorman, LeRoy, 66
Graetz, Carolyn Noah, 111
Granger, Helen A., 100
Greene, Mac, 71
Greene, Steven H., 23
Grognet, Ron, 30
Gurnack, Gwenn, 80
Hafernik, Johnnie Johnson, 69
Hall, Autumn Noelle, 80
Hall, Carolyn, 102
Han, John J., 101
Hansel, Bryan, 79
Hanson, Simon, 35
Hart, William, 31
Harvey, Michele L., 65
Harvey, Patricia M., 46
Haslett, Arch, 98
Hata, Tomoko, 86
Hatley, Anne, 63
Hazelton, Marilyn Shoemaker, 106
Hazen, Elizabeth, 26
Herrin, Poppy, 32
Hinderliter, Carolyn M., 86
Hoagland, Jeff, 87
Hodge, Steve, 103
Hogan, Joanne M., 32
Holzer, Ruth, 25
Hotham, Gary, 91
Howard, Elizabeth, 44
Hoyle, Ginny, 29
Huggett, Elinor Pihl, 84
Hutchison, Connie, 55
Jacobs, David, 9

Jorgensen, Jeanne, 46
Kacian, Jim, 7
Kagan, Oleg, 48
Kennedy, Phillip, 108
Kindelberger, Roy, 69
Kinory, John, 12
Kipps, Mary, 56
Knight, Marylouise, 88
Knoll, Tricia, 71
Koen, Deb, 22
Kolodji, Deborah P., 63
Kozubek, S.M., 50
Lange, Jill J., 89
Lanoue, David G., 63
Larson, Pamela, 12
Laurila, Jim, 10
Lee, Catherine J.S., 44
Lee, Michael Henry, 54
Lee, Phyllis, 77
Lempp, Brenda, 16
Liljedahl, Marcus, 49
Londner, Renee, 21
Longenecker, Gregory, 79
Lovin, Carole Ann, 87
Lucky, Bob, 89
Luke, E., 26
Lukstein, Janis, 75
Lynch, Doris, 26
m., paul, 110
Machmiller, Patricia J., 43
MacQueen, Kate, 23
MacRury, Carole, 50
Magyar, Ann, 90
Mainone, Robert F., 36
Makino, Annette, 100
Manley, CR, 38

Martin, Jeannie, 79
McClintock, Michael, 111
McGee, Margaret D., 78
McHugh, Laureen, 12
McIntosh, Leanne, 67
McKeon, Joe, 105
McMullen, Jeffrey, 75
Mehring, Walt, 105
Merrill, RaNae, 68
Milton, Katherine Raine, 108
Mize, Timothy I., 37
Moeller-Gaa, Ben, 107
Momoi, Beverly Acuff, 43
Montreuil, Mike, 18
Moritz, Ralph, 67
Moss, Ron C., 42
Muirhead, Marsh, 70
Munro, Marie Louise, 56
Nash, Paul S., 47
Newkirk, Mary Ann, 67
Nguyen, Christina, 109
Niedzielska, Suzanne, 56
Noeth, Patricia, 33
Nowaski, Catherine, 70
Odeh, Rita, 16
O'Leary, Karen, 76
Olinger, Ellen Grace, 70
Olson, Marian, 101
Owen, Renée, 31
Packer, Roland, 104
Painting, Tom, 103
Palka, Kathe L., 53
Parsons, John, 30
Paulson, James A., 33
Peckham, Ellen, 65
Penton, Ann M., 58

Pfeffer, Bruce J., 91
Pierides, Stella, 75
Prefontaine, Joan, 85
Pretti, Sharon, 51
Quinnett, John, 72
Rees, Lynne, 54
Rehling, Michael, 105
Richards, Sue, 97
Rielly, Edward J., 10
Robinson, Chad Lee, 41
Rooney, Mary Ellen, 112
Root-Bernstein, Michele, 34
Rosenow, Ce, 64
Ross, Bruce, 50
Rossi, Joan W, 45
Rozmus, Lidia, 112
St. Clair, Richard, 24
Savic, Miloje, 6
Schallberger, Judith M., 84
Schnell, Rich, 34
Schnell, William F., 54
Schoenburg, Michael B., 32
Schwader, Ann K., 73
Shalom, Belle, 88
Sheffield, Michael, 85
Simpson, Gary, 7
Skrivseth, D.W., 111
Skvortsova, Olga, 15
Slesnick, Carole E., 107
Snow, Barbara, 74
Sola, Nicholas M., 109
Sondik, Sheila, 57
Stepenoff, Bonnie, 49
Stillman, Jeff, 92
Stromberg, Karen, 98
Stuart-Powles, Celia, 45

36120839R00074

Made in the USA
Charleston, SC
25 November 2014